YOUR KNOWLEDGE HAS VALUE

Bibliographic information published by the German National Library:

The German National Library lists this publication in the National Bibliography; detailed bibliographic data are available on the Internet at http://dnb.dnb.de .

Imprint:

Copyright © 2016 GRIN Verlag, Open Publishing GmbH
Print and binding: Books on Demand GmbH, Norderstedt Germany
ISBN: 9783668260221

This book at GRIN:

http://www.grin.com/en/e-book/322466/the-vegan-proposition-of-speciesism

Ariel Prince

The Vegan Proposition of Speciesism

GRIN Publishing

The Vegan Proposition of Speciesism

The vegan movement has cultivated a reputation amongst the typical meat-eating individual for their seemingly hostile and unapproachable nature. When noting what some may call their aggressive shaming of those who choose not to involve themselves with a vegan oriented lifestyle, the vegan community has had trouble in gaining traction with non-vegans. While the movement prides itself on their impassioned motivation to put an end to animal cruelty, most crucially in the context of livestock farming, and bringing awareness to all of the social and health benefits of veganism, the support isn't swelling as one might think it would for such a well-intentioned cause. As surprising as some may find, including even activists within the vegan community, a new era of the "classical vegan argument" has introduced a theme that is most commonly rejected by the general population. An emergence in the term 'speciesism[1],' used by vegans of every distinction, has struck a particularly bad chord under the mainstream consensus. In recent years, the societal implications rooted in speciesism have evolved into a chief arguing tool for vegans in their pursuit to expose the speciesist[2] tendencies of the meat-eating community. The speciesist claim is an all-encompassing expression of the negative feelings held towards the livestock industry and all those who support it through their own consumption of meat. Examining 'speciesism' first outside and then within the context of a vegan's argued opposition of the speciesist actions, we will discover clear underlying critical thinking flaws within the movement as a whole. There is a distinct arguable failure in the vegan

---

[1] The assumption of human superiority leading to the exploitation of animals.
The idea that being human is a good enough reason for human animals to have greater moral rights than non-human animals. (BBC)

[2] The action of and individual participating in or contributing to the implied hierarchical structure presented in the argument of speciesism.
Individuals [humans] benefitting from the hierarchy of speciesism while being aware and unwilling to "change."

1

movement's attempts to equate societies questioned speciesist priorities and animal rights violations within the agribusiness industry[3].

Through anti-speciesist arguments, vegans now commonly equate practices in society that are fundamentality different in nature, such as animal cruelty to issues of human rape or slave trade. Although most anyone would see any one of these issues as morally wrong in nature, there has to be a question of the concordance of each of these issues to one another. With groups of individuals spanning from those descended from slave ancestry to rape and molestation victims, there's comes a speculation of these attempted parallels that are definitively damaging the vegan movements advancement. (add more here and speciesism and how it's "part" of common society)

Tobias Leenaert of the Vegan Strategist, in an article attempting to show the "grouping" flaw of distinctive vegan arguments involving the anti-speciesist sentiment by drawing on certain societal issues outside of animal cruelty. Although Leenaert finds the premise of speciesism to be valid and justified by example of modern society, he is quick to acknowledge the shortcomings of the anti-speciesist argument, and provides example of typical flawed vegan arguments:

> When I recommend meat reduction or Meatless Mondays, I get to hear that that is speciesist, because we wouldn't approve of something like Child Abuse Free Mondays in the case of humans. When I advocate that we should try to be gentle and sensible and patient when talking about animal suffering and veganism, I get to here "Would anyone advocate for the abolition, or the regulation, of child sex slavery?" All of us would say it is our moral obligation to advocate for the absolute end of child sex slavery, and that "improvements" are wholly inadequate, and speciesist. (Leenaert)

---

[3] The group of industries dealing with agricultural produce [livestock] and services required in farming.

One may read these conversational examples and think them to be extreme in their comparisons and the truth is, they are extreme. That being said, the "extreme" nature of the counterparts [i.e. child sex slavery] to animal suffering aren't unrealistic in their occurrences, so why when reading this would someone see the typical vegan comparison as off-putting? Leenaert elaborates on his examples by noting that the deep-seeded flaw of this sort of argument is that the vegan community is comparing two social issues that don't lie within the same context in any respect. The argument has accomplished the intended effect of lasting and having memorable intensity, but the argument's negative aspect is in its inability to face a counter-argument by someone of the opposing viewpoint, simply because the comparison, ironically, isn't comparable at all. Leenaert gives another criticism of that same premise of an argument, facilitating the dialogue, "We couldn't tell people to try out a vegan challenge like Veganuary (you can't tell rapists to try to stop raping for a month!)." If the first set of dialogues weren't convincing enough to reveal the flaws in the typical anti-speciesist argument, this point shows another dimension the same flawed argument can hold. The vegan argument of comparison will always find itself to be detrimental; if not by offending individuals who fall into the categories being marginalized [minority races, sexual assault victims], it will discourage involvement in vegan activism efforts by condemning individuals who are making even small strides to make an impact in the movement. Looking at the failings of the anti-speciesist argument, the rippling effects of such a damaging vegan sentiment presented to the public are evident.

The movement's foremost misstep in its presentation of the anti-speciesist argument lies in their Us-vs-Them thinking. As stated by Gerald Nosich, author of *Learning to Think Things Through*, when any one or group of individuals holds the Us-vs-Them mentality that translates into their motivations towards situational approaches, they tend to "vastly oversimplif[y] the

3

complexity of reality." As seen previously in the examples provided by Leenaert, vegan activists are forming a lump sum of circumstantial social issues to compare with animal rights violations, when in any other context, they may have opted for a more realistic approach. Being part of a large social movement, it makes it that much easier for a vegan to attach onto the general views and opinions of their peers and form generalizations that then disregard the complexities of social issues outside of the one they're addressing. Nosich's has a simple response to offer for those suffering from Us-vs-Them thinking: develop and practice "a tolerance for ambiguity and an acceptance of less-than-certain answers."

Vegan anti-speciesists are sometimes guilty of only showing themselves to have and justifications operative as a result of their own individual experiences that were the cause of them living a vegan lifestyle. In this respect, they are demonstrating a complete lack of intellectual empathy towards an individual who may involve themselves in what vegans fight for and against, while at the same time, deciding not to become a vegan. The lifestyle choice just described is a very feasible one, but it is one that is not often considered because of the vegan attitude towards individuals seeking change by other means and methods outside of strict veganism. With little empathy being shown, vegans are shutting themselves off from feeling the entire weight of the outsider's viewpoint that could potentially hold value in its very opposition. This attitude of outsider (non-vegan) ostracism and misuse of the argument of 'speciesism' is detrimental to the movement because it completely limits the movement's potential to gain more active participants. Why should this matter? For a movement such as veganism, ever increasing involvement is what is needed to make a meaningful and lasting impact on the environment. This is the point where vegans have to critically examine what really is the question at issue pertaining to the vegan movement; does a vegan choose animal activism efforts or anti-

4

speciesism, and is there even room for both to sustain themselves? Vegans are fogged in their purpose for the movement on whether their primary intentions are to promoting the agenda of anti-speciesist rhetoric, or to deeper enrich themselves and others in the mission of maintaining animal rights.

The most vocal opposition to the new 'speciesism' argument comes from minority ethnic groups [slave descendants] that see it, in all honesty, as a form of racism. As Claire Heuchan writing with Media Diversified relays it, "This racism [marginalization of minority ethnic groups' struggles], so casually delivered, is designed to add shock value – to trigger a dietary epiphany." Unfortunately for the movement of well-meaning, progressive minded people, their conscious efforts are now being shadowed by their lack of intellectual humility to resign to the fact that they do not hold all solutions to social injustice representation just because they've identified a strong culmination of ethical issues [in animal rights initiatives] that formed their movement; vegan activists haven't reached a place where they are able to fully fight their egocentric mentalities when addressing those individuals outside of the movement.

Because vegans have recently introduced this new method of approach, people on the other end of their "extremist arguments" are feeling as though their problems are being marginalized by what they see as vegans essentially saying, "How can this human social issue be so important when supposed conscious citizens don't even care about the animals that are suffering every day in the meat and dairy industry?"

Sufficiency in execution of the anti-speciesist argument was ignored by the prominent influencers in the vegan movement who didn't take into consideration all of the different elements at play that are responsible for the distinguishing features of all social issues. In order for any issue to be assessed efficiently, all of the layers (being context, frame of reference, etc.)

5

have to be peeled back and examined. In doing this, the anti-speciesist argument through self-analysis could have identified its internal deficiencies and adjusted its approach to the general public in a more inviting and inclusive way while still getting their point across.

Self-justification dawned over the vegan movement's activists when the speciesism proposal unveiled itself. As mentioned in Carol Tavris and Elliot Aronson novel, *Mistakes Were Made (but Not by Me)*, self-justification is merely the act of an individual justifying or excusing his or her own actions. While it may appear as a normal thinking process, self-justification an also manifest itself as a means for individuals to carry out and action, task, or draw claims, based primarily or even purely on their singular intentions. The contradiction vegans have fallen into leading to their mistake of arguing anti-speciesism lies directly in self-justification. Veganism aims to strip you away from all of your previously held beliefs of consuming animals products from birth, one of the only innate traits you've carried consistently throughout life without question. When someone is faced with the choice of becoming a vegan, they can no longer self-justify the reasons for consuming animal products in the present or in the future, and are forced to concede to a different moral standing. Vegans contradict this notion the moment they choose to force the idea of anti-speciesism onto other individuals. They're justifying every reason within themselves of why their way is the best way, while concurrently dismissing all of the viewpoints of all others. While veganism aims to challenge some of "vegan convert's" self-justifying habits, they have really just inadvertently manifested and repacked self-justification where it fits into the aspect of the "moral side of society."

A vegan perspective is needed to gain the contrasting vantage point of an anti-speciesist. As expressed by authors Matthew Cole and Karen Morgan as part of the *2011 Brock Review,* we as humans, particularly here in America, perpetuate the very real and active "human to nonhuman hierarchy." We have cognitively established a scale of moral worth where humans have assigned themselves the maker and manufacturers key, placing human standing above all others, with every other non-human creature tiered beneath us. Cole and Morgan hint at some of the cultural character traits that define a typical non-vegan when presented with the reasonable path of veganism stating that non-vegans are skilled in working under several stages of denial. "A key aspect of denial is that it frequently involves complying with social norms that help to shape individual choices when it comes to either paying attention to or ignoring difficult truths" (Cole, Morgan). The authors are propositioning that maybe it isn't quite the anti-speciesist argument that holds the perpetrators of crimes against critical thinking, but it may very well be those denying their role [non vegans] speciesist systems in society (particularly in the agribusiness industry). Falling into the category of denial and pertaining directly to the correlation of society and anti-speciesism are the listed denials of responsibility, denial of any real harm or injury to any party in the scope of speciesism, and most notable in relation to this analysis, the "condemning of the condemners" (Cole, Morgan).

They authors make an excellent point but the problem in their claims is that the proposal of "societal denial" is not only broad and overreaching (with the argument being based purely from a reaction to the anti-speciesist sentiment only), but one could also argue that denial is as natural and common a trait within an individual at any given time because in many instances, denial stems from lack of knowledge of something to begin with. The grouping of an entire culture under this conception of human to non-human hierarchies is a hard scheme to push considering that most people have never considered speciesism as it pertains to their life dieting habits (if they have even heard of the concept, for that matter).

7

James Liam of the Daily News Service presents the unsuccessful fate of the vegan movement's efforts to consolidate social issues to gain a comparative advantage when arguing a vegan case: The argument of anti-speciesism in relation to other social issues falters as a "misguided attempt to forge facile links between human and animal exploitation. The consequences of the anti-speciesist sentiment as an approach in encouraging a vegan lifestyle don't simply end at the clear faults in critical thinking that have occured within the vegan movement as a whole, but also the direct implications on failure to "make the case" to non vegans on what the vegan lifestyle *really* promotes. The vision of the movement has been clouded by corrupted critical thinking application, and activists are now faced with the decisions of value, purpose, and direction they hold when asking themselves, what *is* and what *can* the vegan movement be?

Works Cited

Cole, Matthew, and Karen Morgan. "Veganism Contra Speciesism: Beyond Debate." Academia.edu. Web. 15 Apr. 2016.

Flinn, Angel, and Dan Cudahy. "Speciesism and Veganism: Transcending Politics and Religion." Gentle World RSS. 28 Nov. 2011. Web. 14 Apr. 2016.

Freeman, and Bluesteel. "Speciesism Is an Unjustifiable Form of Discrimination." Debate: Speciesism Is an Unjustifiable Form of Discrimination. Web. 18 Apr. 2016.

Heuchan, Claire L. "Veganism Has a Serious Race Problem." Media Diversified. Media Diversified, 16 Dec. 2015. Web. 06 Apr. 2016.

James, Liam. "White Veganism: The Vegan Movement's Very Real Race Problem - Daily News Service." Daily News Service. 01 Feb. 2016. Web. 05 Apr. 2016.

Leenaert, Tobias. "When the Term "speciesism" Gets Overused." The Vegan Strategist, 28 Jan. 2016. Web. 05 Apr. 2016.

Nosich, Gerald M. Learning to Think Things Through (LTTT): A Guide to Critical Thinking across the Curriculum. Boston ; Munich: Pearson, 2012. Print.

Tavris, Carol, and Elliot Aronson. Mistakes Were Made (but Not by Me): Why We Justify Foolish Beliefs, Bad Decisions, and Hurtful Acts. Orlando, FL: Harcourt, 2007. Print.